BRANCH LINES TO FALMOUTH HELSTON AND ST. IVES

Vic Mitchell and Keith Smith

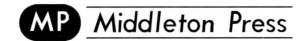

MP Middleton Press

Cover picture: The class 4500 Prairie tanks were used on all three branches for almost 40 years and so a representative must appear on the cover. No. 4561 was recorded in August 1951, approaching Penwithers Junction where the Newham and Falmouth branches leave the main line. It is bound for Newquay. (H.F.Wheeller/R.S.Carpenter)

Published November 2001

ISBN 1 901706 74 5

© Middleton Press, 2001

Design   Deborah Esher
Typesetting   Barbara Mitchell

Published by
            Middleton Press
            Easebourne Lane
            Midhurst, West Sussex
            GU29 9AZ
Tel: 01730 813169
Fax: 01730 812601

Printed & bound by Biddles Ltd,
            Guildford and Kings Lynn

CONTENTS

INDEX

ACKNOWLEDGEMENTS

We are very grateful for the help received from so many of the photographers. Our thanks also go to W.R.Burton, R.M.Casserley, D.Clayton, L.Crosier (Signalling Record Society), G.Croughton, A.Dasi-Sutton, E.W.Fry, M.J.Furnell, P.Hay, F.Hornby, M.A.N.Johnston, J.R.W.Kirkby, N.Langridge, S.C.Nash, P.O'Callaghan, D.T.Rowe, Mr D. and Dr S.Salter, G.T.V.Stacey, E.Wilmshurst, E.Youldon and our ever supportive wives.

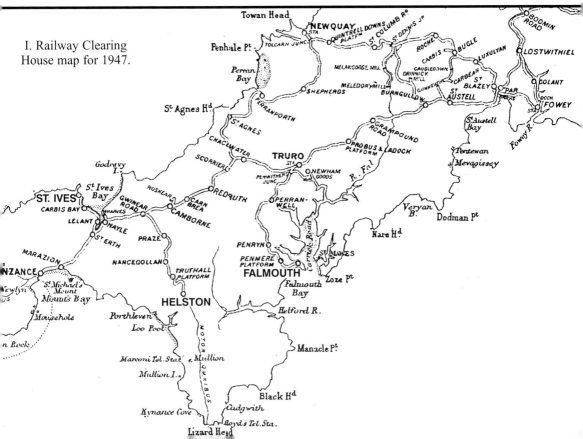

I. Railway Clearing House map for 1947.

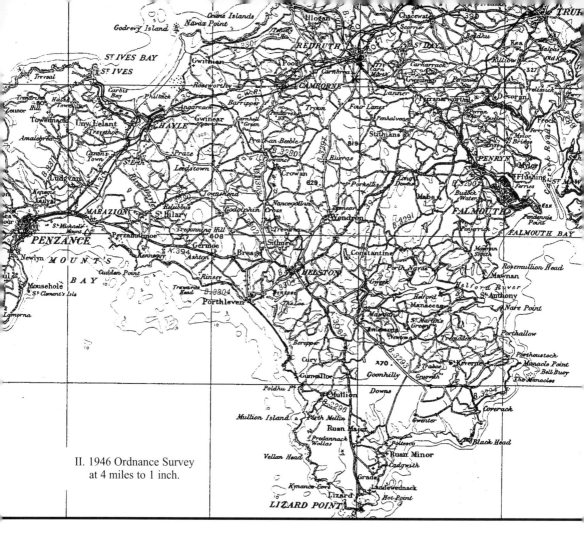

II. 1946 Ordnance Survey
at 4 miles to 1 inch.

GEOGRAPHICAL SETTING

Falmouth Branch

The undulating route crosses a number of valleys and headlands, this originally necessitating eight timber viaducts and two tunnels in only eleven miles. Four of the former were eventually replaced by embankments, the others being rebuilt in concrete thus:

Penwithers	1926	Embankment
Ringwell	1933	Embankment
Carnon	1931	Concrete
Perran	1927	Concrete
Ponsanooth	1930	Concrete
Pascoe	1923	Embankment
Penryn	1923	Embankment
Collegewood	1934	Concrete

The long established town of Falmouth is situated on the estuary of the River Fal, which allowed the development of a substantial dockyard and provision of safe anchorage for large vessels in Carrick Roads. Its sheltered location gave rise to the development of a year-round holiday resort with good bathing and sailing.

Helston Branch

Most of the line is between about 250 and 400 feet above sea level, the former figure applying at each end. This upland area is windswept and thinly populated, of no great interest to holidaymakers. However, the coast of The Lizard peninsular appealed to discerning visitors.

The historic stannary town of Helston (tin marketing centre) had a weekly market and a metropolitan borough status at the time of the branch closure, although the population was only about 7000 souls at that period. The gradient profile shows the irregular nature of the terrain, which has only minor watercourses.

St. Ives Branch

Although only four miles in length, the branch must be one of the most scenically attractive in England. Its spectacular climb along the edge of steep cliffs and its situation on the margin of salt marshes combine to give splendid views across St. Ives Bay and the Hayle Estuary.

The well sheltered resort of St. Ives has a small harbour and is attractively situated among rugged cliffs, which culminate at the impressive St. Ives Head north of the town.

All three branches were constructed largely on Devonian Sandstone which is of little economic value.

The maps are to the scale of 25 inches to 1 mile, unless otherwise shown.

HISTORICAL BACKGROUND

The West Cornwall Railway was established under an Act of 3rd August 1846 to incorporate the Hayle Railway, improve it and extend it east and west. Passenger services between Redruth and Penzance began on 11th March 1852. An extension to Truro (Higher Town) followed on 25th August of that year, with a further extension to Truro (Newham) on 1st April 1855.

The Act for the Cornwall Railway to build a single track broad gauge line from Plymouth to Falmouth was also passed on 3rd August 1846. It was financed jointly by three other railways - the Bristol & Exeter, the Great Western and the South Devon. The consulting engineer was Mr I.K.Brunel. The route between Plymouth Millbay and Truro opened to passengers on 2nd May 1859 and to freight in the following October. It was extended to Falmouth on 24th August 1863 and to the docks in January 1864.

The WCR was converted from standard to broad gauge by the addition of a third rail, following control of the line passing to the "Associated Companies", listed above, in 1866. Broad gauge goods trains began on 6th November of that year and passenger services followed on 1st March 1867. Some goods trains contained wagons of both gauges until total abandonment of the broad gauge on 20-21 May 1892. (A special adaptor wagon separated the two types.)

The Associated Companies were amalgamated in 1876 and thus the GWR had control of the main line and branches thereafter.

The St. Ives branch was authorised on 7th July

1873 and opened on 1st June 1877. It was to be the last broad gauge branch to be completed.

The Helston branch Act was passed on 9th July 1880 and the line came into use on 9th May 1887. It was built to standard gauge and was owned by the Helston Railway Company until 1898, although operated by the GWR from the outset.

Upon nationalisation in 1948, the lines in West Cornwall became part of the Western Region of British Railways.

Unlike the other two branches, the one to Helston was closed: to passengers on 3rd November 1962 (the first in Cornwall) and to goods on 4th October 1964. The goods branch to Newham closed on 8th November 1971.

Privatisation resulted in Prism Rail securing a 7½ year franchise on 13th October 1996 and the remaining two branches were soon operated by trains branded "Wales & West".

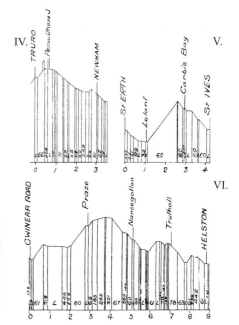

PASSENGER SERVICES

The sample figures quoted relate to down trains running on at least five days per week

Falmouth branch

	Weekdays	Sundays
June 1869	4	2
July 1878	7	2
January 1888	9	3
July 1908	14	3
August 1928	17	7
July 1948	16	8
May 1962	16	9
June 1988	13	8
August 2001	12	10

Helston branch

	Weekdays	Sundays
January 1888	6	0
July 1904	11	2
August 1928	16	0
March 1938	9	0
April 1943	6	0
July 1948	8	0
May 1962	8	0

St. Ives branch

	Weekdays	Sundays
July 1878	8	3
January 1888	8	4
July 1908	14	6
August 1928	16	0
April 1943	10	0
July 1948	13	8
May 1962	15	12
June 1978	20	19
June 1979	24	21
June 1988	24	16
June 2001	22	15

Following the opening of Lelant Saltings "Park & Ride" scheme in May 1978, some trains reversed there instead of St. Erth in the Summer.

1908

TRURO and FALMOUTH.—Great Western.

Miles	Down.	Week Days.															Sundays.		
		mrn	mrn	mrn	mrn	non	aft	aft	aft	aft	aft	aft	aft	aft	aft		mrn	mrn	aft
	Truro ....dep.	6 35	8 25	9 40	1020	12 0	1 38	2 25	3 27	4 18	5 30	6 10	8 0	8 40	1040	....	6 35	10 5	6 8
4¼	Perranwell	6 45	8 35	9 50	1032	1210	1 50	2 37	3 36	4 30	5 40	6 20	8 10	8 50	1050	....	6 45	1015	6 20
8¼	Penryn	6 55	8 45	10 0	1042	1220	2 0	2 49	3 46	4 40	5 50	6 30	8 20	9 0	11 0	....	6 55	1025	6 30
11¾	Falmouth, for St. Mawes ..arr.	7 3	8 55	1010	1052	1230	2 8	2 57	3 57	4 50	6 0	6 40	8 30	9 10	1110	....	7 3	1035	6 39

Miles	Up.	Week Days.															Sundays.		
		mrn	mrn	mrn	mrn	mrn	mrn	mrn	aft	aft	aft	aft	aft	aft	aft		mrn	aft	aft
	Falmouth ....dep.	7 10	7 45	8 35	9 10	1015	11 0	1135	1245	2 40	3 40	5 20	7 0	7 50	9 20	....	8 55	3 10	5 20
3½	Penryn	7 19	7 53	8 45	9 19	1025	11 8	1144	1255	2 48	3 48	5 30	7 8	7 59	9 30	....	9 5	3 20	5 30
7½	Perranwell	7 28	8 2	8 55	9 29	1035	1118	1152	1 5	2 58	3 58	5 40	7 18	8 8	9 40	....	9 15	3 30	5 40
11¾	Truro 22, 27 ....arr.	7 39	8 13	9 5	9 39	1044	1128	12 3	1 15	3 8	4 8	5 50	7 29	8 20	9 50	....	9 25	3 39	5 50

1888

HELSTON and GWINEAR ROAD.—Great Western.

Up.	gov	mrn	aft	aft	aft	gov
Helston ....dep	9 40	1135	1 48	4 35	6 40	7 48
Nancegollan	9 51	1148	1 59	4 46	6 51	7 59
Praze	9 57	1155	2 5	4 52	6 57	8 5
GwinearRd. 19, 18 arr	10 5	12 5	2 13	5 0	7 5	8 13
PENZANCE 18..arr	1045	1242	2 50	6 25	....	8 45
PLYMOUTH 19.. "	1 50	....	6 5	8 10	1026	....

	gov	mrn	mrn	aft	aft	1&2
Millbay Station, PLYMOUTH 18 dep	6 50	9 20	11 0	2 35	....	6 5
PENZANCE 19 "	10 0	....	2 5	....	6 35	gov
Gwinear Road ...dep	1037	1250	2 45	6 7	7 15	8 38
Praze	1045	1 1	2 53	6 15	7 23	8 46
Nancegollan	1051	1 10	2 59	6 21	7 29	8 52
Helston ....arr	11 2	1 21	3 10	6 32	7 40	9 3

1908

GWINEAR ROAD and HELSTON.—Great Western.

Miles	Down.	Week Days.										Sundays.		
		mrn	mrn	mrn	aft	aft	aft	m	aft	m	aft	mrn	aft	
	Gwinear Road...dep.	7 10	8 55	1110	1240	3 15	4 50	5 20	7 5	7a25	9 20	7 10	5 35	....
2¼	Praze	7 18	9 2	1117	1247	3 23	4 58	5 28	7 12	7a33	9 28	7 18	5 43	....
5	Nancegollan	7 24	9 8	1124	1254	3 29	5 4	5 34	7 18	7a39	9 34	7 24	5 49	....
7	Truthall Platform....	....	9 16	....	1 1	....	....	5 40	7 25	7a45	....	....	....	....
8¾	Helston ‖ ....arr.	7 35	9 24	1135	1 9	3 40	5 15	5 48	7 33	7a53	9 45	7 35	6 0	....

Miles	Up.	Week Days.										Sundays.		
		mrn	mrn	m	mrn	mrn	aft	aft	aft	m	aft	mrn	aft	
	Helston....dep.	6 30	7 55	9 50	1025	1155	1 55	4 10	5 55	6a25	8 35	6 30	4 55	....
1¾	Truthall Platform..	....	8 0	....	....	12 0	....	4 15	....	6a32	8 40	....	....	....
3¾	Nancegollan	6 41	8 8	10 1	1036	12 8	2 5	4 23	6 6	6a39	8 48	6 41	5 6	....
6	Praze ....[27	6 47	8 14	10 7	1043	1214	2 12	4 29	6 12	6a45	8 54	6 47	5 12	....
8¾	Gwinear Road. 22,	6 55	8 22	1015	1052	1222	2 21	4 38	6 20	6a53	9 2	6 55	5 20	....

a Mondays, Fridays, and Saturdays. **m** Motor Car, one class only. ‖ Station for Porthleven (2¼ miles), Mullion (6 miles), The Lizard (10 miles), Kynance Cove (10 miles), Housel Bay (10½ miles), Cadgwith (9½ miles), and Coverack and St. Keverne (10½ miles).

GWINEAR ROAD and HELSTON

WEEK DAYS ONLY

Miles		am		am			am			pm			pm			pm		pm		pm		
—	**Gwinear Road** .. .. dep	**7 45**	..	**8 30**	..	..	**10 55**	..	..	**2 10**	..	..	**4 11**	..	..	**4 50**	..	**8 5**	..	**9 25**	..	..
2¼	Praze	7 55	....	8 37	....	....	11 3	....	....	2 17	....	....	4 19	....	....	4 58	....	8 13	....	9 33	....	....
5¼	Nancegollan	8 2	..	8 43	..	..	11 8	..	..	2 24	..	..	4 26	..	..	5 3	..	8 18	..	9 38	..	..
7	Truthall Platform	....	....	8 49	....	....	11 15	....	....	2 31	....	....	4 32	....	....	5 10	....	....	....	9 44	....	....
8¾	**Helston** .. .. .. arr	**8 20**	..	**8 55**	..	..	**11 20**	..	..	**2 37**	..	..	**4 38**	..	..	**5 15**	..	**8 30**	..	**9 50**	..	..
—	The Lizard ¶ .... arr	....	....	1022	....	....	1 19	....	....	5 8	....	....	6 22	....	....	7 29	....	9S57	....	....	....	....

Miles		am			am			am			pm			pm			pm			pm			
	The Lizard ¶ .. dep	..	..	..	8† 3	..	..	10 25	..	.	1 22	..	..	..	..	..	5 11	..	..	7 32	..	..	..
—	**Helston**........... dep	**7 45**	....	....	**9 50**	....	....	pm **1 10**	....	....	**3 30**	....	....	**4 10**	....	....	**7 3**	....	....	**8 45**	....	....	....
1¾	Truthall Platform	7 51	..	..	..	..	..	..	..	.	3 37	..	..	4 17	..	..	7 10	..	..	8 51	..	..	..
3½	Nancegollan	8 2	....	....	10 3	....	....	1 22	....	....	3 44	....	....	4 25	....	....	7 16	....	....	8 58	....	....	....
6	Praze	8 8	..	..	1010	..	..	1 30	..	.	3 50	..	..	4 31	..	..	7 23	..	..	9 4	..	..	..
8¾	**Gwinear Road** .... arr	**8 16**	....	....	**1017**	....	....	**1 38**	....	....	**3 57**	....	....	**4 38**	....	....	**7 30**	....	....	**9 12**	....	....	....

¶ By "Western National" Omnibus. Heavy luggage not conveyed. Connecting services are also run between Helston Station and Mullion Cove, etc.

S Saturdays only. Applies daily from 11th June, 1962. † Does not run on Bank Holidays

1962

1878

ST. ERTH and ST. IVES.—Great Western.

Mls.	**St. Erth**	5 45	8 0	1030	1220	2 40	4 10	7 5	9 50	...	Sndy	8 0	4 10	6 20
1	Lelant..	6 48	8 3	1033	1223	2 44	4 13	7 8	9 53	....		8 3	4 13	6 23
3	Carbis B	6 56	8 11	1041	1231	2 52	4 21	7 16	10 1	....		8 11	4 21	6 31
4½	**St. Ives.**	7 0	8 15	1045	12 35	2 56	4 25	7 20	10 5	....		8 15	4 25	6 35
Mls	**St. Ives**	6 20	7 35	9 50	1155	2 0	3 40	6 30	9 20	....	Sndy	6 45	3 40	5 50
1¼	CarbisB	6 24	7 39	9 54	1159	2 4	3 44	6 34	9 24	....		6 49	3 44	5 54
3¼	Lelant .	6 32	7 47	10 2	12 7	2 12	3 52	6 42	9 32	....		6 57	3 52	6 1
4½	**St. Erth**	6 35	7 50	10 6	1210	2 16	3 55	6 45	9 35	....		7 0	3 55	6 5

ST. ERTH and ST. IVES.—Great Western

Mls	**Down.**	**Week Days.**									**Sundays.**			
		mrn	gov	mrn	aft	aft	aft	gov	gov		mrn	gov	gov	gov
—	**St. Erth** ....dep	7 30	1033	1132	1230	2 43	5 15	6 55	8 50	....	7 30	8 40	1045	6 15
1	**Lelant**	7 33	1036	1135	1233	2 47	5 18	6 59	8 53	....	7 33	8 43	1049	6 18
3	**Carbis Bay**	7 41	1044	1142	1241	2 55	5 26	7 7	9 1	....	7 41	8 51	1056	6 26
4½	**St. Ives** ....arr	7 45	1048	1145	1245	2 59	5 30	7 11	9 5	....	7 45	8 55	11 0	6 30
Mls	**Up.**	gov	gov	mrn	mrn	aft	aft	gov	gov		mrn	gov	gov	aft
—	**St. Ives** ....dep	6 20	9 50	11 5	1158	2 0	4 50	5 50	8 12	....	7 0	8 15	1020	4 50
1¼	**Carbis Bay**	6 24	9 54	11 9	12 1	2 4	4 54	5 54	8 16	....	7 4	8 19	1024	4 54
3¼	**Lelant**	6 32	10 2	1117	12 9	2 12	5 2	6 2	8 24	....	7 12	8 27	1032	5 2
4½	**St. Erth 19, 18**	6 35	10 6	1120	1213	2 16	5 5	6 5	8 27	....	7 15	8 30	1035	5 5

1888

1988

St. Erth — St. Ives

Mondays to Fridays

Miles																										
—	Penzance 135 d	06 37	.....	*07 20*	08 38	*08 55*	10 07	.....	*10 40*	.....	*11 50*	13 02	.....	.....	*14 30*	15 24	.....	*16 25*	.....	*17 30*	18 10	.....	*19 05*	*20 05*	*20 45*	.....	.....
0	**St. Erth** d	06 45	07 30	07 59	08 46	09 25	10 15	10 45	11 16	11 48	12 18	13 10	13 41	.	14 42	15 32	.	16 36	.	17 43	18 18	18 50	19 26	20 15	20 56	.	.
¾	Lelant Saltings ¶ d	.....	.....	.....	.....	09 28	10 18	10 48	11 19	11 51	12 21	13 13	13 44	14 09	14 45	15 35	16 01	16 39	17 05	17 47	.....	18 53	19 29	20 18	.....	.....	.....
1	Lelant d	06 48	07 33	08 02	08 49	.	.	.	11 21	.	.	13 15	.	.	.	15 37	.	16 41	.	17 49	18 21	.	19 31	20 20	20 59	.	.
3	Carbis Bay d	06 53	07 38	08 07	08 54	09 34	10 24	10 54	11 26	11 57	12 27	13 20	13 50	14 15	14 51	15 42	16 07	16 46	17 11	17 54	18 26	18 59	19 36	20 25	21 04	.....	.....
4½	**St. Ives** a	06 56	07 41	08 10	08 57	09 37	10 27	10 57	11 29	12 00	12 30	13 23	13 53	14 18	14 54	15 45	16 10	16 49	17 14	17 57	18 29	19 02	19 39	20 28	21 07	.	.

Saturdays

Penzance 135 d	07 00	*07 35*	*08 00*	09 20	.....	*09 58*	10 45	*11 17*	11 54	.....	*12 30*	13 12	*13 45*	*14 01*	.....	*15 02*	*15 45*	16 35	*17 20*	.....	18 05	.....	19 27	*20 05*	.....	*20 45*	.....
St. Erth d	07 10	07 45	08 20	09 28	.	10 18	10 53	11 28	12 02	.	12 40	13 20	13 55	14 35	.	15 13	16 03	16 49	17 33	.	18 13	18 52	19 35	20 15	.	20 56	.
Lelant Saltings ¶ d	.....	.....	.....	09 31	.....	10 21	10 56	11 31	12 05	.....	12 43	13 23	13 58	14 38	.....	15 16	16 06	16 52	17 36	.....	18 16	18 55	19 38	20 18	.....	.....	.....
Lelant d	07 13	07 48	08 23	09 33	.	.	10 58	.	12 07	.	.	.	14 00	14 40	.	15 18	16 08	16 54	17 38	.	18 18	18 57	19 40	20 20	.	20 59	.
Carbis Bay d	07 18	07 53	08 28	09 38	.....	10 27	11 03	11 37	12 12	.....	12 49	13 29	14 05	14 45	.....	15 23	16 13	16 59	17 43	.....	18 23	19 02	19 45	20 25	.....	21 04	.....
St. Ives a	07 21	07 56	08 31	09 41	.	10 30	11 06	11 40	12 15	.	12 52	13 32	14 08	14 48	.	15 26	16 16	17 02	17 46	.	18 26	19 05	19 48	20 28	.	21 07	.

Sundays

Penzance 135 d	08 56	09 47	.....	.....	.....	.....	12 22	.....	.....	.....	14 09	.....	.....	15 27	.....	.....	.....	.....	18 12	.....	.....	.....	.....	.....	.....	.....	.....
St. Erth d	09 04	09 55	.	10 33	11 42	.	12 30	.	.	13 28	14 17	.	.	15 35	.	16 45	17 20	.	18 20	19 09	.	19 47	20 19	.	.	.	.
Lelant Saltings ¶ d	09 07	09 58	.....	10 36	11 45	.....	12 33	13 01	.....	13 31	14 20	.....	14 47	15 38	.....	16 48	17 23	.....	18 23	19 12	.....	19 50	20 22	.....	.....	.....	.....
Lelant d	09 09	.	.	.	.	.	12 35	.	.	.	14 22	.	.	.	.	.	17 25	.	.	19 14	.	19 52	.	.	.	.	.
Carbis Bay d	09 14	10 04	.....	10 42	11 51	.....	12 40	13 07	.....	13 37	14 27	.....	14 53	15 44	.....	16 54	17 30	.....	18 29	19 19	.....	19 57	20 28	.....	.....	.....	.....
St. Ives a	09 17	10 07	.	10 45	11 54	.	12 44	13 10	.	13 40	14 30	.	14 56	15 47	.	16 57	17 33	.	18 32	19 22	.	20 00	20 31	.	.	.	.

1. Falmouth Branch
TRURO

VII.   The 1906 survey at 6ins to 1 mile has the main line from Plymouth at the top and its continuation on the left. The Falmouth branch is shown near Penweathers, as is the viaduct which stood until 1926. To the right of it is the Newham branch, which curves off the bottom of the page to reappear near the right border. Note that the main station was still on the edge of Truro.

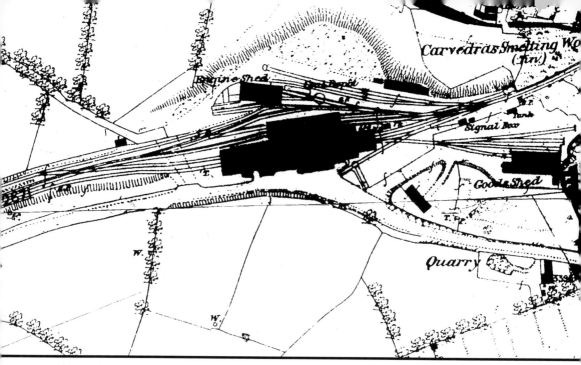

VIII. The first edition features the overall roof which lasted until the late 1890s. The dotted lines across the tracks west of the station indicate the position of a level crossing that was in use until about 1876. From top to bottom on the left is a broad gauge siding, the standard gauge WCR (the survey must have been carried out before 1867) and the CR's main line to Falmouth.

1.   The rebuilding of the station was completed as shown on this postcard which was produced soon afterwards. The extension to the 1874 goods shed is evident, as is a Royal Mail van. The concept of multiple insulators on the arms of telegraph poles had not yet arrived. Truro became the county town of Cornwall in 1888, when Cornwall County Council was formed. (Lens of Sutton)

2.   The level crossing was replaced by a footbridge which was used by the producers of this photograph and nos. 3, 4, and 9. The four-wheeled coaches on the right are in the bay platform created in 1912. The engine shed was in the left background until 1899, at which time most Falmouth trains used the centre through line. (Lens of Sutton)

3.   A 1920 panorama includes the 1914 platform lengthening and two bogie coaches in the bay platform for local services. The water columns were later moved to the ends of the platform extensions. (LGRP/NRM)

4.   A westward view in the late 1930s includes the 1900 engine shed and the 1897 49-lever West Box. The line on the left had been only a dock siding until 1912. The adjacent track was designated "down main", the next was "up branch" and the one at platform 1 was "up main", until 1971. (R.S.Carpenter coll.)

5.   The public footbridge can be seen beyond West Box on 26th September 1956. On shed that day were 0-6-0PT no. 9434 and no. 1007 *County of Brecknock*. Steam traction ceased here in March 1962 and part of the shed was adapted for diesel servicing. (H.C.Casserley)

6.	The 11.15am to Falmouth departs from the bay behind 0-6-0PT no. 4622 on 8th April 1960, as no. 4083 *Abbotsbury Castle* waits with a down van train. West Box was in use until 7th November 1971. (R.C.Riley)

7.	Many Falmouth trains used "up branch" until the track remodelling that was completed on 7th May 1971. It was then renamed "up main" and platform 4 became "up bay", but is now trackless. A class 118 DMU waits to leave for Falmouth at noon on 15th June 1967. (G.Gillham)

8.   The noon branch departure waits at platform 1 on 20th February 1973 as no. 1723 arrives with the 08.00 Bristol to Penzance. Above its coaches is a glimpse of the station's second footbridge, a feature that befits a city, a status that Truro has had since 1877. (D.H.Mitchell)

9.   Departing for Falmouth on 2nd May 1987 is no. 142022. These "Skipper" units proved unsuitable for the curvaceous West Country lines and were soon sent elsewhere. In the background is the depot of Cornwall Farmers Ltd which had its own siding in use for artificial fertiliser traffic until about 1996. Diesel servicing ceased in 1965 and the goods yard handled only full loads after 1971. (P.G.Barnes)

10.   A typical branch train stands at the bay on 1st April 1998. On the west wall of the shed on the left is a cabinet containing a release instrument for the single line staff for the branch. (M.J.Stretton)

Other views of this station can be found in pictures 20 to 31 in our *St. Austell to Penzance* album. Penwithers Junction and Newham are also included therein.

WEST OF TRURO

11.   No. 50013 *Agincourt* draws the 09.20 Liverpool to Penzance through the 70 yard Higher Town tunnel on 25th April 1984. The unusual signal on the right, controlling the Falmouth branch junction, seems to have been constructed from an old semaphore signal post with the colour light and junction indicators bolted on as separate units. The tunnel originally had two single lines: the WCR on the left and the CR on the right, the tracks being of different gauges. (G.Gillham)

12.   Seen at the same location in August 1951 is no. 6968 *Woodcock Hall* with a down express. The eastern terminus of the WCR was situated on the left of this view from 1852 to 1855, after which period trains ran to Newham instead. The tunnel was completed in 1859. (H.F.Wheeller/R.S.Carpenter)

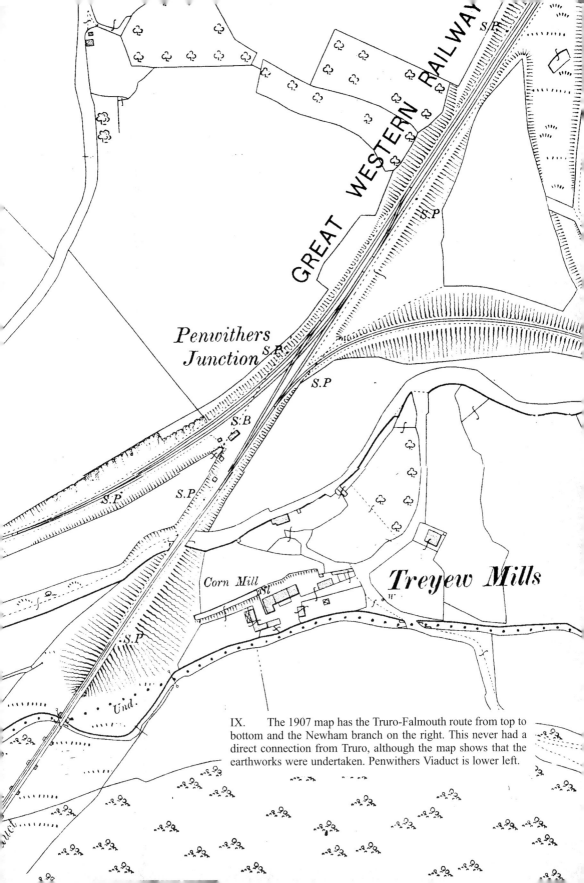

GREAT WESTERN RAILWAY

S.P.

S.P.

Penwithers
Junction S.P.

S.P.

S.B.

S.P.

S.P.

S.P.

S.P.

Corn Mill

Treyew Mills

Und.

IX.   The 1907 map has the Truro-Falmouth route from top to bottom and the Newham branch on the right. This never had a direct connection from Truro, although the map shows that the earthworks were undertaken. Penwithers Viaduct is lower left.

13.   DMU no. LA500 proceeds towards Falmouth on 18th August 1969, the main line curving to the right. The Newham branch is to the left of the 36-lever signal box; both closed on 7th November 1971. The box was built in 1893 and the loop was lengthened in 1913. (N.L.Browne)

14.   After the signal box closed, up branch trains used the down main line to Truro, as witnessed on 20th February 1973. Note the track alterations and also the presence of a catch point, a well proven safety feature that is being widely abandoned and could have prevented many recent disasters. The WCR line to Newham originally crossed the Falmouth branch on the level. (D.H.Mitchell)

15.   Penwithers Viaduct was in the vicinity of the fresh ballast in the background of the previous picture. It is seen in 1926, during the construction of an embankment that would eliminate it. The locomotive appears to be a Simplex of the type used in the battlefields of World War I. (M.Dart coll.)

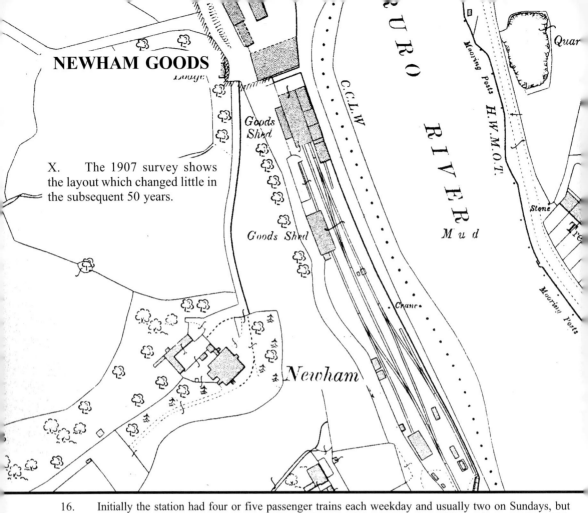

NEWHAM GOODS

Lodge

Goods
Shed

X.   The 1907 survey shows
the layout which changed little in
the subsequent 50 years.

Goods Shed

Newham

C.C.L.W

T R U R O   R I V E R

M u d

Crane

Mooring Posts   H.W.M.O.T.

Quar

Stone

Tre

Mooring Posts

16.   Initially the station had four or five passenger trains each weekday and usually two on Sundays, but after 1859 there was only one out in the morning and one back in the evening. This service ceased on 16th September 1863 and the building was used for goods thereafter. This view is probably from the 1930s, when there was usually a staff of three men. (British Railways)

17.   A siding was provided for the South West Gas Board in April 1955, almost ½ mile from the end of the 2¼ mile long branch. It was in use until 25th December 1970 and was photographed on 16th December 1961. Beyond the gate there were two parallel lines, linked by two crossovers. (L.Crosier)

18.   No. 5552 was recorded on the quay alongside the Truro River in the early 1950s. The crane was of 3-ton capacity. The short siding ending at the buffers was removed in 1965. (H.Davies)

19. The handling of domestic coal here relieved pressure on the main goods yard, which had been extended several times. No. 7422 waits with three brake vans on 14th August 1956. (H.Davies)

20. The terminal building is seen on the same day. On the right is a warehouse towards the south end of which ran a siding until about 1900. There had been an engine shed at the south end of the site in the early years. (H.Davies)

21.   Sparnock Tunnel is 491yds long and is seen on 28th April 1983 as the 17.40 from Falmouth proceeds north. It is about to descend at 1 in 66. (T.Heavyside)

Newham	1903	1913	1923	1933
General goods forwarded (tons)	9520	18992	4330	1502
Coal and coke received (tons)	904	1994	1159	381
Other minerals received (tons)	1425	1719	2210	2962
General goods received (tons)	5116	8188	8602	11030
Trucks of livestock handled	-	2	-	-
(* not available.)				

22.	Carnon Viaduct was one of the last timber structures in Cornwall to be rebuilt. Work started in 1931 and the replacement opened on 13th August 1933. The 1826 Redruth & Chacewater Railway passed under the branch on the floor of the valley on its way to the quay at Devoran. (R.S.Carpenter coll.)

23.	The new structure is 258yds in length and has brick arches surmounted by concrete blocks and parapets. The piers of its predecessor are evident as no. P467 works the 18.10 from Truro on 28th April 1983. (T.Heavyside)

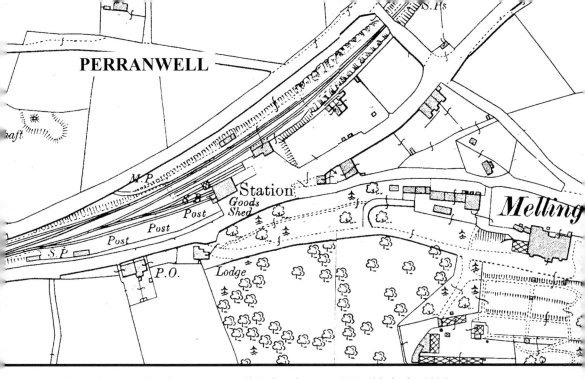

PERRANWELL

Station
Goods
Shed

Melling

M.P.

Post

Post

Post

Post

S.P.

P.O.

Lodge

XI.   The station was simply "Perran" until 19th February 1864. This is the 1906 survey.

24.   We start our visit to this station with three views from August 1948. It is situated on a headland between deep valleys and is in a cutting at the Falmouth end and on made ground at the other (see next picture). No. 5526 is about to pass over Carnon Viaduct. (J.H.Moss/R.S.Carpenter)

25.   The cattle dock (right) was added in 1907 and an extra siding was provided beyond it in 1920. The mess for the track gang was a former broad gauge coach and is visible near the signal. (J.H.Moss/R.S.Carpenter)

26.   One of the three short sidings on the down side was filled, probably with empties. The wooden wagons had received many odd boards during World War II and their original owner's identity had thus been lost. (J.H.Moss/R.S.Carpenter)

27.   A foot crossing on a sharp bend was a dangerous feature, but there were few fast trains to present a problem. This and the next view date from September 1966. There had been a camping coach located here in the Summers of 1936-39 and 1952-64. (P.J.Kelley)

28. The 21-lever signal box of 1894 remained in use until 18th April 1966, when the up sidings and loop were taken out of use. The goods yard closed to general traffic on 4th January 1965, but some occasional sugar beet and flower traffic continued for another two years. (P.J.Kelley)

29. Class 108 2-car set no. 956 leaves for Truro on 23rd April 1992. Staffing had ceased on 6th May 1968 and the building became a residence. (G.Gillham)

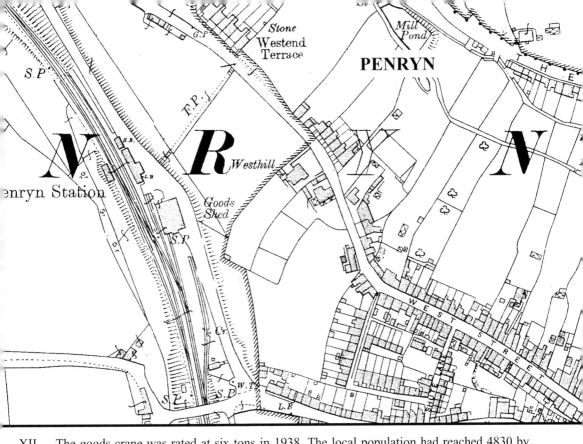

XII. The goods crane was rated at six tons in 1938. The local population had reached 4830 by 1961. This is the 1906 edition.

30. A down train passes over the foot crossing as a group of locals wait to take the short journey to Falmouth. The wide space between the tracks is a legacy of the broad gauge days. The 1894 signal box is near the locomotive and is visible below the canopy. (Lens of Sutton)

31.   Work started in 1922 to reduce the track curvature, lengthen the loop and provide more sidings. Part of a goods train stands on the up line as its engine shunts the siding. (LGRP/NRM)

32.   The new platforms are complete, but unlit, and a walkway has been built across the old running lines, suggesting that the date is 24th June 1923, the day that the new layout came into use. The point in the foreground was for one of two new sidings at the north end of the site. (Lens of Sutton)

33.   Two more new sidings (left) were provided at the south end, together with a cattle dock. The down side building was subsequently remote from the platform. Unlike its predecessor, the up side shelter (right) was hip-roofed. There were camping coaches based here in 1934-38. (M.Dart coll.)

34.　　A short train arrives from Falmouth in August 1948 and passes the end of the headshunt. Its elevated position at the end of the level sidings indicates the severity of the branch gradient. (J.H.Moss/R.S.Carpenter)

35. Unlike the original platforms, the 1923 pair were straight and closer together. This June 1956 view features 0-6-0PT no. 8421 bound for Falmouth. The 32-lever signal box (to the right of the camera) was in use until 7th November 1971. (J.W.T.House/C.L.Caddy)

36. Falmouth-bound (despite the destination blind) is class 108 DMU set no. 956 on 23rd April 1992. A car park occupies the site of the goods yard, which closed on 8th November 1971. The two northern sidings remained usable until 1979. (G.Gillham)

37.   An early 20th century postcard features another splendid fan-type viaduct and also the small town of Penryn, which once had a busy commercial harbour. Penryn Viaduct was to the north of the station and was eliminated in 1923; this one was almost half a mile south thereof and was named Collegewood. (M.Dart coll.)

38.   Collegewood Viaduct was rebuilt in 1934, using mainly concrete blocks. Its length is 300 yds. The gradient is 1 in 59 up towards Truro, both sides of Penryn station. (M.Dart coll.)

PENMERE

39.   Passenger traffic commenced on 1st June 1925, the term "Platform" being used by the GWR to denote a staffed halt. This northward view includes a loop that came into use in 1940 to serve a fan of four sidings behind the camera. They were in a Ministry of Defence oil depot, which was closed in March 1967. (E.W.Goslin coll.)

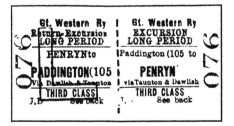

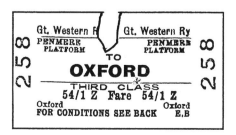

40.	The prospective passenger's perspective was recorded in August 1958. The facility is much used by residents of the western side of Falmouth. (L.W.Rowe)

41.	After years of neglect, a group of local residents formed the Friends of Penmere Station and set about restoring its dignity. A brick shelter was built and its roof trimmed with a traditional valence. The work resulted in the receipt of a national award in September 2000. The photograph is from April 2001. (M.Turvey)

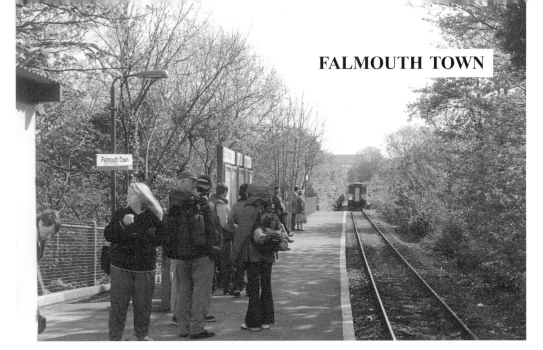

FALMOUTH TOWN

42.   A new branch terminus was established at Avenue Road, close to the town centre, on 7th December 1970. The platform components had previously been in use at Perranporth Beach Halt. Initially called "Falmouth", it was renamed "The Dell" on 5th May 1975 when the original terminus was reopened. It was changed, yet again, to "Falmouth Town" on 3rd October 1988. The gradient is 1 in 79 up for no. 150233 which is arriving from Falmouth Docks. Due to this incline, trains terminating here had to run south (empty) onto level track to enable the driver to change ends in complete safety. (M.Turvey)

FALMOUTH DOCKS

43.   The location of this turntable is shown in the centre of map XIII. The line in the left foreground continued to the goods shed, while its neighbour, and two others, acted as short end-loading sidings. The locomotive was an Avonside Engine Company product and was photographed in 1890, two years before the broad gauge was abandoned. (LGRP/NRM)

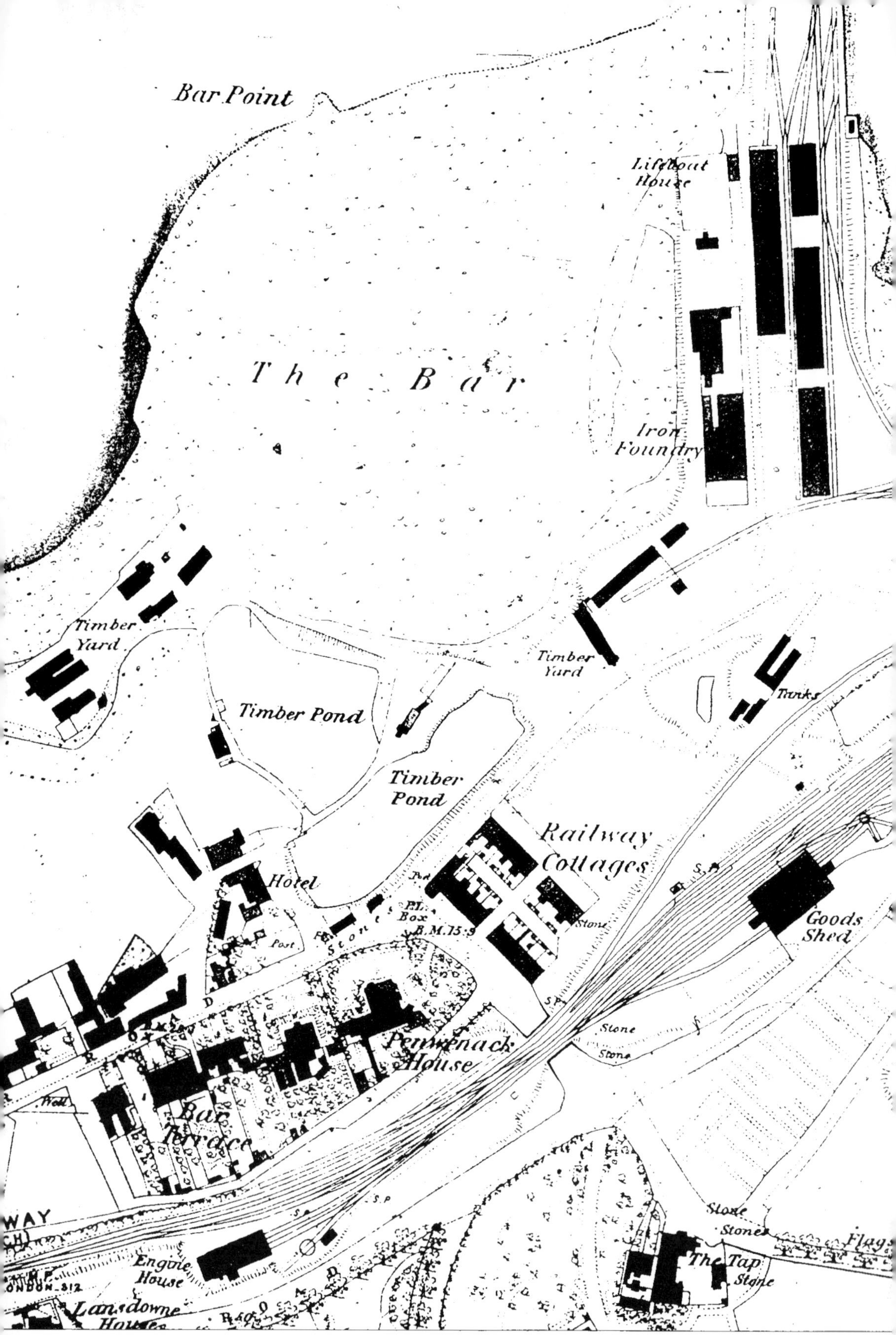

Bar Point

The Bar

Lifeboat House

Iron Foundry

Timber Yard

Timber Pond

Timber Yard

Tanks

Timber Pond

Railway Cottages

Goods Shed

Hotel

P.L. Box

B.M.15.9

Post

Stone

S.B.

Stone

Stone

Stone

Penwinnick House

Bar Terrace

Well

Stone

Stones

Flag

The Tap

Stone

WAY

CH)

Engine House

ONDON 312

Lansdowne Houses

ROAD

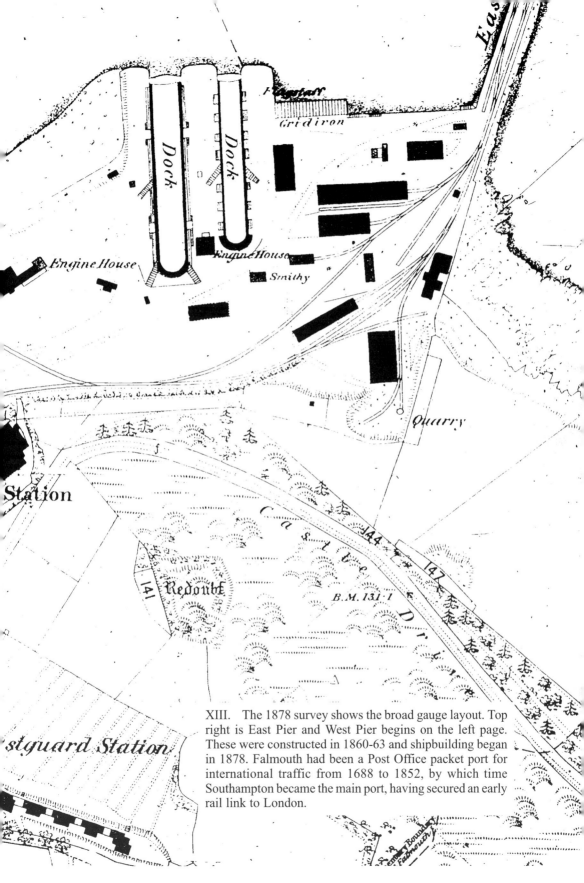

Dock

Dock

Flagstaff

Gridiron

Engine House

Engine House

Smithy

Quarry

Station

Castle Drive

144

143

141

Redoubt

B.M. 131·1

stguard Station

XIII. The 1878 survey shows the broad gauge layout. Top right is East Pier and West Pier begins on the left page. These were constructed in 1860-63 and shipbuilding began in 1878. Falmouth had been a Post Office packet port for international traffic from 1688 to 1852, by which time Southampton became the main port, having secured an early rail link to London.

44.   An 1895 panorama of Carrick Roads has three goods sidings in the foreground (only two are visible) and three tracks between the two passenger platforms. Some sheeted wagons stand on the line to the dockyard, which descends on a steep gradient. (LGRP/NRM)

45.   The entrance was on the south-east elevation and was recorded by an early postcard producer. The overall roof gave a fitting ambience for the terminus of the CR whose trains started under a similar structure at Plymouth Millbay. (Lens of Sutton)

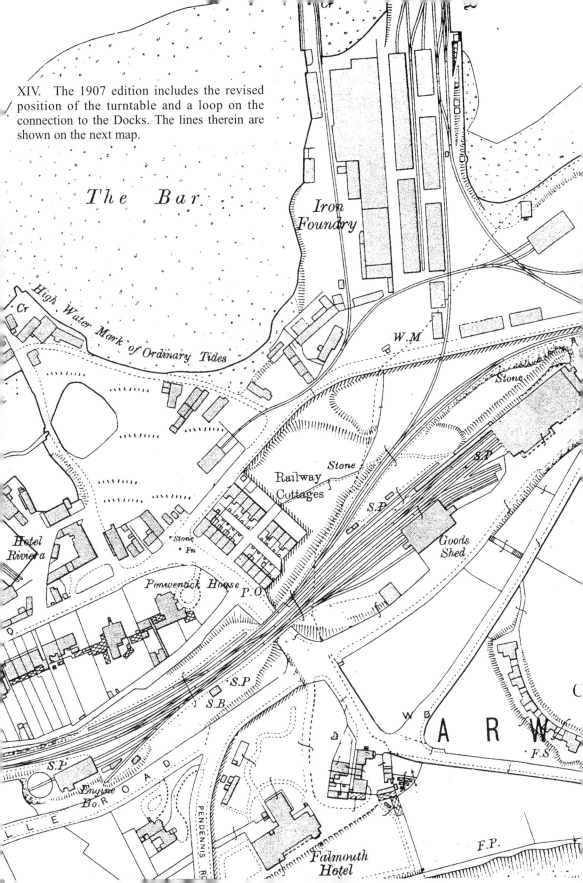

XIV. The 1907 edition includes the revised position of the turntable and a loop on the connection to the Docks. The lines therein are shown on the next map.

The Bar

Iron Foundry

High Water Mark of Ordinary Tides

W.M

Stone

Railway Cottages

Stone

S.P.

S.P.

Goods Shed

Hotel Riviera

Stone Fn

Penwentick House

P.O.

S.P.

S.B.

W

A R W

F.S.

S.P.

Engine Ho.

PENDENNIS ROAD

Falmouth Hotel

F.P.

Cr

46. A 1920 photograph reveals the short length of the up platform. Owing to this handicap, the down platform was signalled for departures from 16th February 1928. Pendennis Castle surmounts the hill on the right. (LGRP/NRM)

47. In the left background is the engine shed, which closed on 21st September 1925. The locomotive is a 3521 class 4-4-0. A down train is arriving some time before the addition of the up starting signal. (Lens of Sutton)

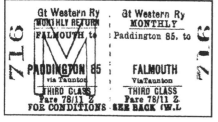

48. A view towards the terminus in 1948 includes the inspection pit and water column that had once stood outside the engine shed. (J.H.Moss/R.S.Carpenter)

49.   No. 5526 is about to create a splendid echo under the ancient roof in August 1948. The down platform canopy extension appears in this picture and in no. 47. (J.H.Moss/R.S.Carpenter)

50.   A June 1956 photograph features 0-6-0PT no. 8421 with a van attached to a short up train. The impressive roof had gone in the early 1950s. (J.W.T.House/C.L.Caddy)

51.   The relative lengths of the platforms are clear in this record of no. 8485 waiting with the 2.25pm to Truro on 26th September 1956. Also evident are the new canopies. (H.C.Casserley)

52.   A view in the other direction on 15th May 1956 includes no. 4574 shunting. In the distance is the signal box which had 41 levers and closed on 27th February 1966, leaving just two ground frames to control the loop points. (M.Mensing)

53.   Close to the six-ton crane on 17th May 1956 is a container that has been lifted off the flat wagon. As in broad gauge days, there were three end-loading docks, the reason not being recorded. No. 5500 has arrived with the 10.50am from Newquay, which was combined with the 12.3pm from Truro on Sundays. (M.Mensing)

54.   Camping coach no. W9905W was in use on 22nd June 1962. One such holiday refuge appeared here also in 1963-64, but not in other years. A rarity arrived on 17th October 1965: a complete Pullman boat train. (J.H.Meredith)

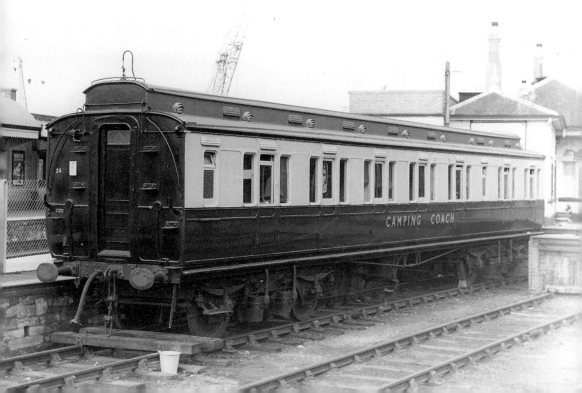

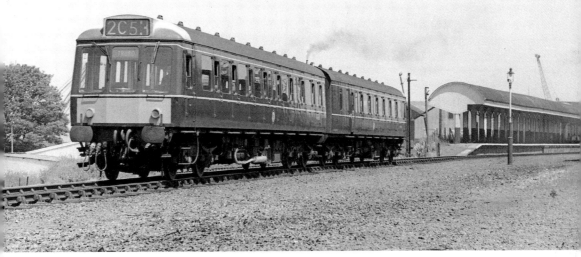

55.   A smart class 118 DMU departs on 15th June 1967. The goods yard had closed on 4th January 1965 and the station would become unstaffed on 6th May 1968, just as the holiday season was starting. The station was closed from 5th December 1970 to 5th May 1975. The suffix "Docks" was added on 3rd October 1988. (G.Gillham)

56.   Redevelopment of the site was beginning when no. 150233 was recorded near the end of the shortened platform on 28th April 2001. The line had been shortened by moving the buffers level with the canopy extension. (M.Turvey)

FALMOUTH DOCKYARD

XV.   We use this heading to distinguish this section from that relating to the station. The Docks had undergone several changes of ownership by the time that shipbuilding ceased in 1930. Extensive ship repair work was undertaken in both wars and this activity developed greatly. The dry docks were completed thus: No. 1 in 1861, No. 2 in 1863, No. 3 in 1921 and No. 4 in 1928, much track alteration being required. On the left is the 1907 edition and the copy on the right is from 1933. Both maps are at about 16ins to 1 mile.

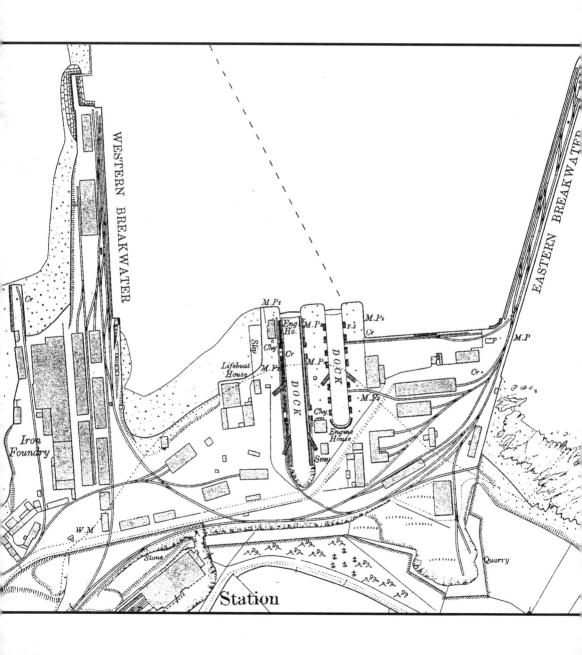

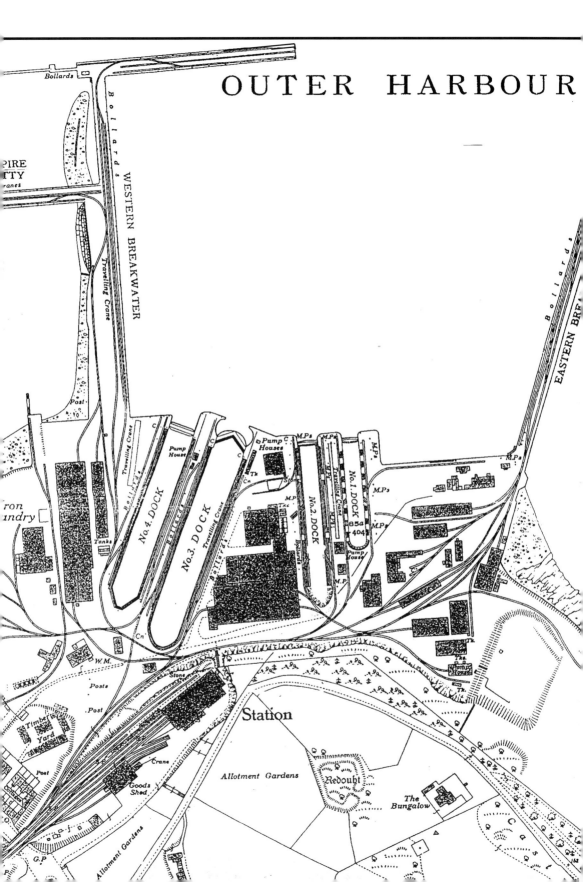

57.   The Falmouth Docks Company bought three vertical boilered 0-4-0s from Sara & Burgess, but these had to be regauged when the dock lines were narrowed in 1892. Four 0-4-0STs from Hudswell Clarke followed in the 1920s. This is no. 5, a 1929 Hawthorn Leslie purchased in 1961 and pictured on 26th June 1962. (J.H.Meredith)

58.   No. 5 is seen at work on the same day near No. 2 Dock. Steel plates and materials of all types were conveyed around the site, but commercial cargoes were insignificant here. (J.H.Meredith)

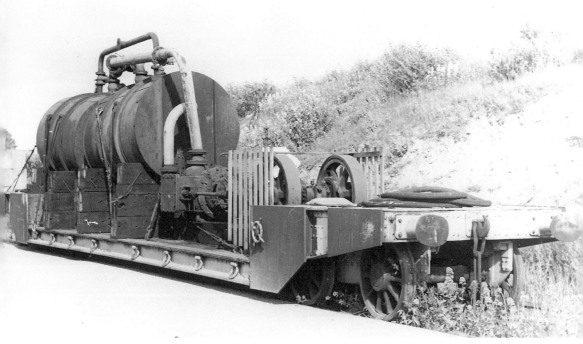

59.   The Docks came to specialise in the cleaning and repair of the interiors of oil tankers, the deep water allowing access for very large vessels. This unusual vehicle carries a large pump for use in such activities. Another specialist task is the treatment of foul water from the washing of ships bottoms. (J.H.Meredith)

60.   Two photographs from 16th June 1977 include Hudswell Clarke no. 3 of 1926, which worked here until 22nd August 1986. It was claimed to be the last steam engine on a dock railway in Britain and it later moved to the Plym Valley Railway. Steel plates stand near the steam crane. (T.Heavyside)

61.   Diesel and electric cranes flank no. 3 in the year of nationalisation. The labour force was soon cut from 1400 to 175 and traffic from BR ceased early in 1980. However some containers of coal were conveyed in July 1997 and the connection is still retained. A Rolls Royce engined Sentinel, built in 1963, was obtained in 1978 and the Docks were denationalised in 1985. This diesel was little used and was sold in 1995, when still numbered 195. (T.Heavyside)

2. Helston Branch

GWINEAR ROAD

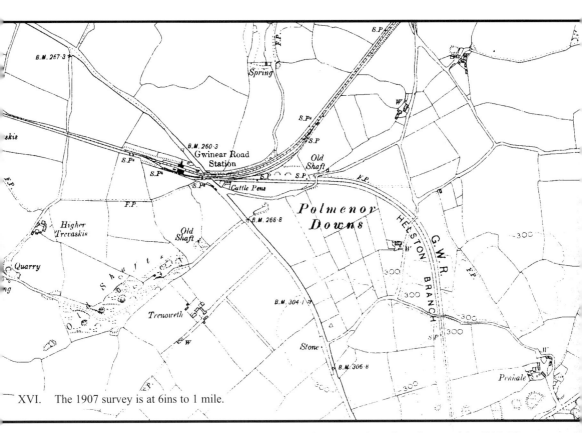

XVI.   The 1907 survey is at 6ins to 1 mile.

62.   There was only a small station and a passing loop before the Helston branch opened in 1887. These buildings were erected at that time, as was the signal box (left) but that lasted only until 1915. The footbridge was built a few years before. The distant arm is white and red, not the familiar black and yellow.   (Lens of Sutton)

63.   The west elevation of the down side building was recorded on 26th September 1956 as passengers changed to the branch train, which had arrived behind 2-6-2T no. 4566. It would use the down main line to run round its train. (H.C.Casserley)

64.   The signal box was moved to the island platform in 1915. It was termed "West Box"; "East Box" was at the far end of the sidings in the left background. No. 4563 arrives with a stopping train for Penzance on 18th August 1958. (E.Wilmshurst)

65.   A goods train from Helston rattles over the level crossing on 29th August 1958. There had been a ticket collecting platform to the right of the vans until 1903. The massive level crossing gates were moved by means of a wheel in the signal box. (L.W.Rowe)

66.   From left to right is the up loop, the double track to Camborne, the down refuge siding and eight parallel sidings. From 1887 to 1892, there were only three and a transfer shed. The Helston branch is in the centre distance and the wagons on the right stand close to the cattle dock and the stationmasters house. (J.H.Moss/R.S.Carpenter)

67.   No. 4574 waits to leave for Helston not long before passenger services were withdrawn on 5th November 1962. This station closed on 5th October 1964 and West Box followed on 31st October 1965, by which time the branch and all the sidings were disused. Little now remains. (R.S.Carpenter coll.)

Other views of this junction and its sidings can be seen in pictures 65 to 72 in our *St. Austell to Penzance* album.

PRAZE

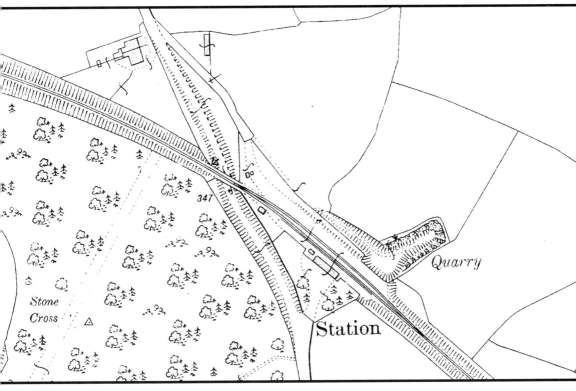

XVII. The station was situated nearly half a mile south of the crossroads at Praze an Beeble and is shown on the 1906 revision.

68.   The station opened with the line, its name simply meaning "Meadow". The photograph gives a false impression; there were usually only two men here until 1930 and one thereafter. Nos 34 and 35 were built especially for the Helston branch as 0-4-2STs and rebuilt as 0-4-4ST/WT in 1895 as shown. (Lens of Sutton)

69.   The goods loop is seen in 1920. It became a siding in about 1950, when the southern points were removed. It was usable until the end of branch freight service, although the site was unstaffed. (LGRP/NRM)

Praze	1903	1913	1923	1933
Passenger tickets issued	8551	10306	8073	4821
Season tickets issued	*	*	62	84
Parcels forwarded	904	2083	1700	2592
General goods forwarded (tons)	86	89	154	146
Coal and coke received (tons)	692	772	25	290
Other minerals received (tons)	26	47	197	90
General goods received (tons)	589	694	339	118
Trucks of livestock handled	-	61	18	2
(* not available.)				

Nancegollan	1903	1913	1923	19
Passenger tickets issued	9239	10819	9272	52
Season tickets issued	*	*	39	
Parcels forwarded	10513	6796	8675	124
General goods forwarded (tons)	343	599	985	14
Coal and coke received (tons)	490	530	131	
Other minerals received (tons)	75	836	104	
General goods received (tons)	993	1219	945	4
Trucks of livestock handled	67	204	130	
(* not available.)				

70.　　The guard waits for the photographer to picture the ground frame on 18th August 1958. This was totally protected from the weather, whereas passengers had no shelter if the waiting room was locked, but at least they had a small amount of paving. (A.E.Bennett)

71.　　Severe weather was recorded on 3rd March 1962 towards the end of a particularly bad period. Unlike most water tanks, this one had no "fire devil" to prevent it freezing. There is now no evidence of a station having been on the site, but the bridge abutments can be seen on the B3303. (P.W.Gray)

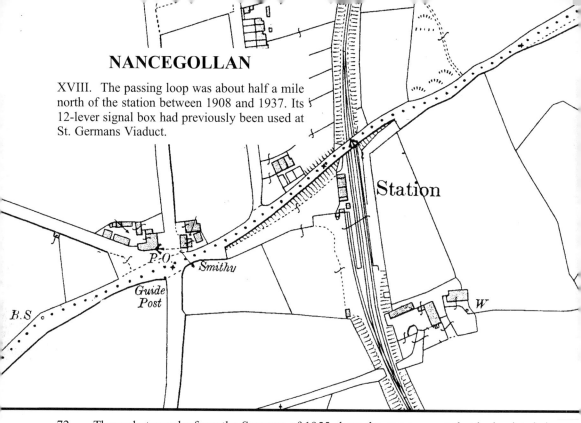

NANCEGOLLAN

XVIII. The passing loop was about half a mile north of the station between 1908 and 1937. Its 12-lever signal box had previously been used at St. Germans Viaduct.

P.O

Smithy

Guide Post

B.S

Station

W

72.   Three photographs from the Summer of 1955 show the arrangement that had existed since 1937, when a passing loop and three sidings were installed. The platform and building on the left came into use at that time, the previous solitary one becoming the up platform, seen in the foreground. (J.H.Moss/R.S.Carpenter)

73.   The three new sidings were laid almost parallel to the up platform, but the western one was removed in 1944 to permit the laying of four curved ones (right) for military traffic. There were five men engaged here throughout the 1930s. (J.H.Moss/R.S.Carpenter)

74.   The 30-lever signal box was in use from 19th September 1937 until 8th October 1964 and was situated at the north end of the up platform. The stone arch was over the running lines and the steel span was added in 1937 to go over the new track leading to the sidings. (J.H.Moss/R.S.Carpenter)

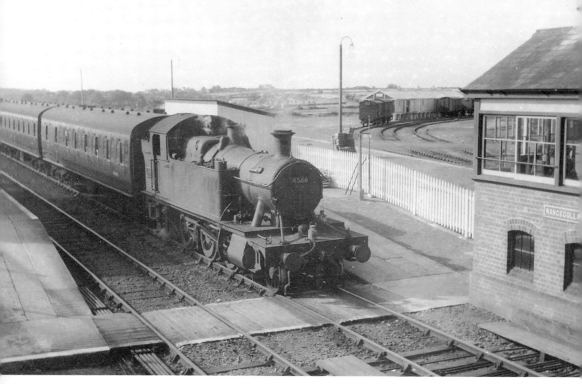

75. Seen from the original bridge in 1957 is no. 4566 bound for Gwinear Road. There was one camping coach parked here in the Summers of 1958-62. The new sidings were required for the growing traffic in broccoli and potatoes. In 1937 alone, an amazing 35,490 tons of the former left Cornwall by rail. (M.Dart coll.)

76. No. 4570 waits on 19th October 1959 while parcel traffic is dealt with on the down platform. The name is pronounced Nancy Gollan, with a hard G, it meaning "Valley of the whet stone". Only the bridges now remain, plus one lamp post. (R.S.Carpenter coll.)

TRUTHALL HALT

77. The halt came into use on 1st July 1905 and was the subject of an official photograph in 1920. It was the guard's duty to provide and remove the oil lamps as appropriate. (LGRP/NRM)

XIX. The halt was almost two miles by train from the end of the line, but not on the route that a crow would take. The 1946 edition at 1ins to 1 mile includes the curving Lowertown or Cober Viaduct (121 yds long) which down trains approached at 1 in 63 and sometimes sped round despite the 35mph speed limit on the branch.

78. Seen near the end of its life, when the sleeper edging was rotting, the halt had an additional lamp with lenses. Its purpose was to assist drivers find the structure at night. There was little habitation nearby. (Lens of Sutton)

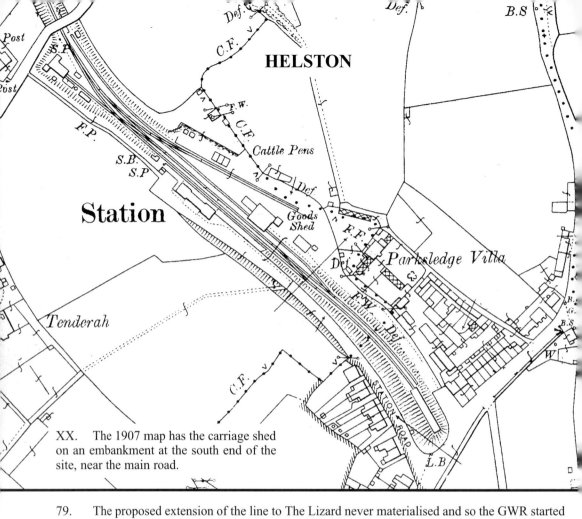

HELSTON

Station

Tenderah

Cattle Pens

Goods
Shed

Parksledge Villa

XX.   The 1907 map has the carriage shed
on an embankment at the south end of the
site, near the main road.

79.   The proposed extension of the line to The Lizard never materialised and so the GWR started
a bus service on 17th August 1903, the first of several. Four vehicles were employed and Royal Mail
was carried on the 11 mile journey. From 1910, the buses replaced trains on Sundays on the branch.
(Lens of Sutton)

80.　　A GWR bus service between Helston and Porthleven began on 2nd October 1909, two "motor cars" being allocated to the four-mile long route. About two miles south of Helston, the local community erected this waiting shelter in 1921. (M.Dart coll.)

ROAD MOTOR-CAR SERVICES.

Between HELSTON AND THE LIZARD.

TO THE LIZARD.

			WEEK DAYS ONLY.	
			a.m.	a.m.
HELSTON (Station)	dep.		7 45	11 45
DODSON'S GAP (for G'nwallo')	,,			
CURY CROSS LANES (for Cury)	,,			
PENHALE (for Mullion) ...	,,	CALLING AT THESE PLACES IF REQUIRED.		
RUAN CROSS ROADS (for Cadgwith)	,,			
HOUSEL ROAD				
THE LIZARD	arr.		9 0	12 55

FROM THE LIZARD.

			WEEK DAYS ONLY.	
			a.m.	p.m.
THE LIZARD	dep.		9 15	4 15
HOUSEL ROAD	,,			
RUAN CROSS ROAD (for Cadgwith)	,,			
PENHALE (for Mullion) ...	,,	CALLING AT THESE PLACES IF REQUIRED.		
CURY CROSS LANES (for Cury)	,,			
DODSON'S GAP (for G'nwallo')	,,			
HELSTON (Station)	arr.		10 25	5 30

XXI. 1904 bus timetable.

81. In the distance in this southward view is the carriage shed which stood until 1957. The diamond crossover on the right was removed in 1915. Note the unusually close proximity of two catch points. (Lens of Sutton)

Helston	1903	1913	1923	1933
Passenger tickets issued	36006	73606	30383	15189
Season tickets issued	*	*	48	71
Parcels forwarded	22566	42864	47005	85962
General goods forwarded (tons)	1456	1745	2071	2043
Coal and coke received (tons)	1941	3096	2292	3549
Other minerals received (tons)	164	1335	1112	1465
General goods received (tons)	4213	6334	6204	4094
Trucks of livestock handled	741	1114	784	618

(* not available.)

82.   The line to the engine shed is lower right in this 1948 view. The 1915 alteration allowed locomotives to run direct from the shed onto coaches standing in the platform. The crane was rated at six tons; there was a two-ton model in the goods shed. (J.H.Moss/R.S.Carpenter)

83.   The building was similar to that at St. Ives and it contained the single line staff instrument in the early years. A Wolseley is parked alongside and in the background is a bus of Western National, a firm part-owned by the GWR until 1948. (J.H.Moss/R.S.Carpenter)

84.   The canopy provided shelter for the full length of the east elevation and often protected large amounts of goods despatched by passenger train, such as dead rabbits for the dinner tables of the Midlands. (Lens of Sutton)

85.   The refreshment room was let out and privately operated. There was a staff of 11 here in 1903, but there were 22 men for most of the 1930s. The Fleet Air Arm station brought additional traffic after it opened in April 1947, one mile south of Helston. (Lens of Sutton)

Gt. Western Ry   Gt Western Ry
HELSTON   HELSTON
              TO
GWINEAR ROAD
9d THIRD CLASS 9d
Issued subject to the conditions & regulations set
out in the Company's Time Tables Rule & Notices
Gwinear Road   Gwinear Road

86.   The signalman collects the staff from an arriving train and will soon place it in his electric instrument. The 21-lever frame was installed in 1958. A second engine can be seen in the shed. (J.H.Moss/R.S.Carpenter)

87.   No. 4540 departs sometime in the mid-1950s and is about to pass the site of the ticket platform, which was in use until 1903. Thereafter, tickets were collected at Nancegollan for many years. (J.H.Moss/R.S.Carpenter)

88.   No. 4588 is in the shed and no. 4574 is on the loop in this 1960 view. The starting signal is "off" and below it is a shunt signal. Cattle wagons (right) were regularly used for the conveyance of broccoli. (R.S.Carpenter coll.)

89.   The siding on the left appears in picture 81, but not in no. 87. It was reinstated in about 1958 for stone traffic. No. 4570 was recorded on 25th June 1962. Only the goods shed still stands and now houses elderly people. (J.H.Meredith)

90.   Diesels of the North British Type 2 appeared only during the final year or so of passenger services on the branch. No. D6326 is about to run round on 21st August 1962. No. D6312 hauled the last train. (J.H.Aston)

3. ST. IVES BRANCH
ST. ERTH

XXII.   The 6ins to 1 mile map of 1890 has the GWR main line from Hayle to St. Erth across the middle, with the St. Ives branch on the left. The track to it from St. Erth was mixed gauge from 1888 to 1892. It had closed by 1918.

91.   This 1920 panorama of the junction includes two unusual features: palm trees and broccoli baskets, both reflecting the mild local climate. The station had been named "St. Ives Road" until the branch opened in 1877, St. Erth village being about a mile south-east of the junction. (LGRP/NRM)

92.   "Metro" class 2-4-0T no. 1496 waits with a train for St. Ives on 28th June 1924. This type of locomotive was used only rarely on the branch after about 1910, 2-6-2Ts of the 4400 and 4500 classes being the norm. (K.Nunn/LCGB)

93.   No. 4574 shunts the small goods dock on 30th August 1956. The crossover was used after the arrival of every train from St. Ives, as the branch was too steep for push-pull working. It was removed in 1969, made redundant by the advent of DMUs. (N.L.Browne)

94.   No. 4545 is on the branch service on 27th September 1956 and is standing near the 1900 platform extension. The sidings in the foreground were used mainly for the berthing of coaches at peak holiday times. (H.C.Casserley)

95.   The low wall to the right of the boys reflects the height difference at the west end of the platforms, due to the main line being on a gradient. On the left is Primrose Dairy, which despatched milk tankers daily to sidings at Kensington Olympia. The chalked notice shows the Summer 1958 frequency. The goods yard closed on 1st May 1967. (A.E.Bennett)

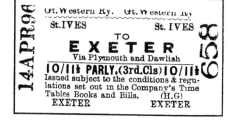

96.   This 1958 photo reveals that Diana Dors was in Plymouth, no doubt generating extra passenger traffic. The different inclination of the platforms resulted in an asymmetric roof over them. The loop and platform 1 had been added in 1894. (E.Wilmshurst)

97.	A DMU is departing for St Ives, as indicated by the signal adjacent to the six-wheeled milk tanker. The service is the 12.33 on 12th September 1973. There had been a double track connection to the main line until October 1964. (D.H.Mitchell)

98.	The 14.47 from Penzance runs onto the branch connection on 2nd May 1987. There were no through passenger services in the reverse direction between 1964 and 1988. Some signalling alterations were made near the crossover at the west end of the station to eliminate this limitation. The class 142 "Skippers" were short lived on the branch. (P.G.Barnes)

Other views of this station can be seen in pictures 81 to 93 in our *St. Austell to Penzance* album.

99.	The single-car class 153s proved ideal for the route, no. 153303 being recorded on 27th April 2001. The signal box has a 69-lever frame dating from 1929 and faces the two former berthing sidings retained by the engineers. (M.Turvey)

15

LELANT SALTINGS

100.   To ease road traffic congestion in St. Ives, a car park for 300 vehicles was built here alongside a new platform which opened on 27th May 1978. A charge of 60p was made and all passengers travelled free. An impressive 136,000 people travelled up to September and by May 1979 the platform length was doubled to take four coaches. There was increased train frequency and the fee was raised to £1. A class 153 unit runs alongside the saltings (salt marshes) on 27th April 2001. (M.Turvey)

May 1983 timetable on Mondays to Fridays

St. Erth and St. Ives (Second Class only)																												Until 30 September
																												A
135 Penzance .. d	06 28	07 40	..	08 27	09 33	..	10 20	..	..	11 55	..	..	..	..	13 45	..	..	..	16 25	..	..	..	18 15	..	..	..	..	21 35
St. Erth .... d	07 18	07 50	08 25	09 07	09 43	10 12	10 41				12 08	12 41			13 41		14 40			16 37	17 12	17 46	18 18	18 51	19 25	20 00	21 00	21 50
Lelant Saltings ¶ d				09	10 09	10 46	10 15	10 44	11	11 30	12 11	12 44	13	13 44	14	14 43	15 08	15 35	16 02	16 40	17 15	17 49	18 21	18 54	19 28	20 03	21 03	21 53
Lelant .... d	07 21	07 53	08 28	09 12															16 42				18 23	18 56		20 05		
Carbis Bay .... d	07 27	07 59	08 34	09 18	09 52	10 21	10 50	11 17	11 44	12 17	12 50	13 17	13 50	14 17	14 49	15 14	15 41	16 08	16 48	17 21	17 55	18 29	19 02	19 34	20 11	21	09	21 59
St. Ives .... a	07 30	08 02	08 37	09 21	09 55	10 24	10 53	11 20	11 47	12 20	12 53	13 20	13 53	14 20	14 52	15 17	15 44	16 11	16 51	17 24	17 58	18 32	19 05	19 37	20 14	21 12	22 02
																												A
St. Ives ..... d	07 33	08 05	08 52	09 25	09 58	10 27	10 57	11 24	11 50	12 24	12 57	13 24	13 57	14 24	14 55	15 21	15 48	16 15	16 55	17 28	18 02	18 35	19 08	19 42	20 25	21 25	22 30
Carbis Bay ..... d	07 37	08 09	08 56	09 29	10 02	10 31	11 01	11 28	11 54	12 28	13 01	13 28	14 01	14 28	14 59	15 25	15 52	16 19	16 59	17 32	18 06	18 39	19 12	19 46	20 29	21 29	22 34
Lelant .... d	07 42	08 14	09 01	09 34	..	..													17	17		19 17		20 34	21 34		
Lelant Saltings ¶ d					11 a07	11 a34	12 01	12 35	13 a07	13 35	14 a07	14 35	15 a05	15 a31	15 a58	16 24	17 04	17 39	18 13	18 46	19 20	20 19	21 37	22 41
St. Erth.. a					10 38		12 07	12 37	..	13 37	..	14 37	..			16 28	17 08	17 45	18 18	18 50	19 22	19 55	20 39	21 37	22 43
135 Penzance... a	07 58	08 35	..	10 43	..	..	12 32	..	..	14 40	..	..	..	16 42	..	17 55	18 36	..	19 59	..	20 57	22 01	23 04

A 18 July to 2 September	b Fridays dep. 22 10, Lelant Saltings 22 19, Carbis Bay 22 19. St. Ives arr. 22 22
	a Until 15 July and from 5 September

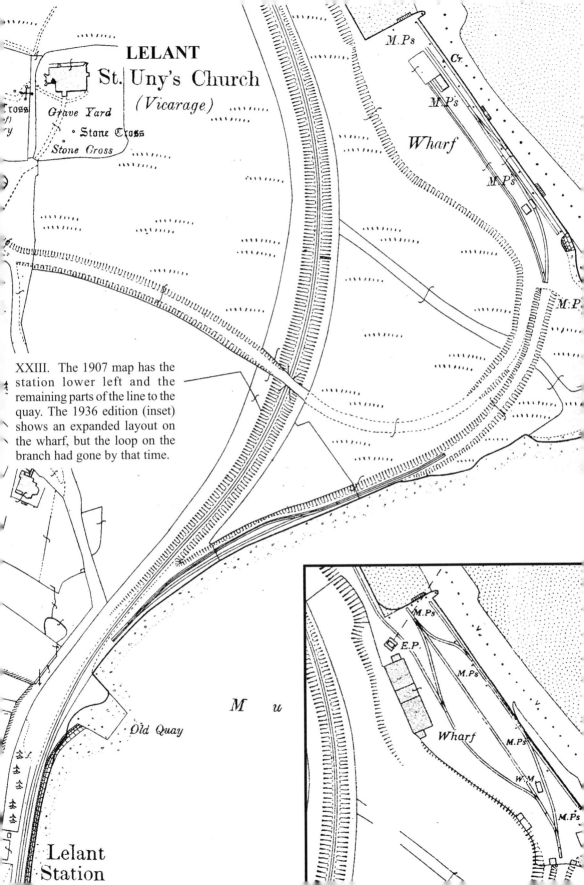

LELANT

St. Uny's Church

(Vicarage)

Grave Yard

• Stone Cross

Stone Cross

Wharf

M.Ps

Cr.

M.Ps

M.Ps

M.P.

XXIII. The 1907 map has the station lower left and the remaining parts of the line to the quay. The 1936 edition (inset) shows an expanded layout on the wharf, but the loop on the branch had gone by that time.

M   *u*

• *Old Quay*

M.Ps

E.P.

M.Ps

Wharf

M.Ps

W.M.

M.Ps

**Lelant
Station**

101.   There was a staff of two at this tranquil location until 1930; thereafter there was one man until staffing ceased on 29th September 1958. The quay branch had been close to the wall on the right. (Lens of Sutton)

———————➤

102.   Unusually, a wooden building was provided, probably due to the difficulty in creating adequate foundations for a stone structure so close to the shoreline. There were three waiting rooms, one for each class. (Lens of Sutton)

———————➤

EMIGRANTS TICKET
Lelant   Lelant
M.R.P   Parly 3rd.Cl.
LIVERPOOL G.W.
via Severn Tunnel, Hereford, Shrewsbury
Wrexham & Woodside Ferry
25/0 PARLY. 3TH RD CLASS 25/0
Liverpool G.W.   Liverpool G.W.
SEE BACK
028

103.   A top-hatted officer oversees the recording of his staff and the inevitable youthful onlookers. There was a signal box behind the camera from 1877 to 1894, when it became a ground frame. (Lens of Sutton)

104.   A generous station yard was provided, but the only goods traffic handled was that which could go by passenger train. The term "halt" was applied from 1958 to 1969, goods handling having ceased in 1956. (Lens of Sutton)

105.   To reduce line occupation, no. 4549 is travelling back from St. Ives attached to no. 4566 on 14th July 1961. The train of gleaming coaches reflects the shimmering water at high tide at this peaceful spot. (P.W.Gray)

106.   The platform had been lengthened on the right in 1894, while the building had been extended more recently to form a dwelling. Bearing Network SouthEast livery, unit no. L842 was remote from its normal habitat on 19th March 1994. (D.H.Mitchell)

107.   This unit is seen in GWR chocolate and cream livery, whch was applied at the time of the
150th anniversary of that company. It is working the 17.25 from St. Ives on 3rd May 1995 and above
its rear cab is Lelant Quay. In the background is Hayle and the viaduct carrying the main line.
(G.Gillham)

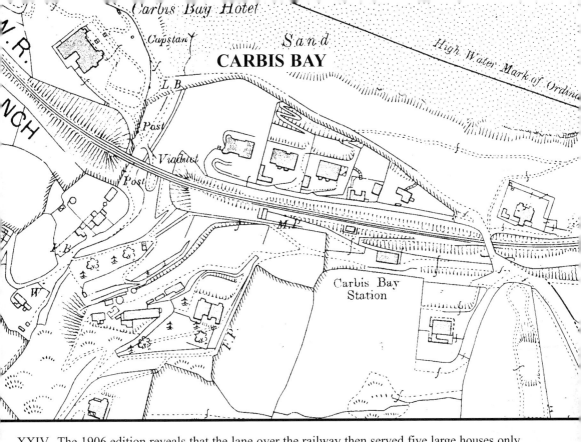

XXIV. The 1906 edition reveals that the lane over the railway then served five large houses only.

108.　To minimise excavation, the main building was built at the top of the cutting and a waiting room provided at platform level. The bridge carried a lane that descended to the beach and which also served an hotel. Two men were employed here throughout the 1930s, but three previously. Staffing ceased in 1956. The locomotive is one of the "Buffalo" class. (Lens of Sutton)

109.   A panorama from the road bridge in 1920 includes the small goods shed at the end of the platform. It was used for parcels traffic until 1956; it also housed passengers' bicycles. The viaduct appears in this and the next picture. (LGRP/NRM)

110.   The platform is not visible in this view from the cliff top on 30th April 1983, but the white fencing above it is. No. P467 is descending at 1 in 60, having left St. Erth at 16.37. There is a speed limit of 20mph along the cliff edge. (T.Heavyside)

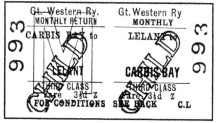

111.   Locomotives have seldom visited the branch since 1962, but on 19th March 1994 nos. 50050 and 50007 worked the "Cornish Caper" with no. 50033 at the far end. The new houses on the right were followed by more to interrupt the passenger's view in 2001. (D.H.Mitchell)

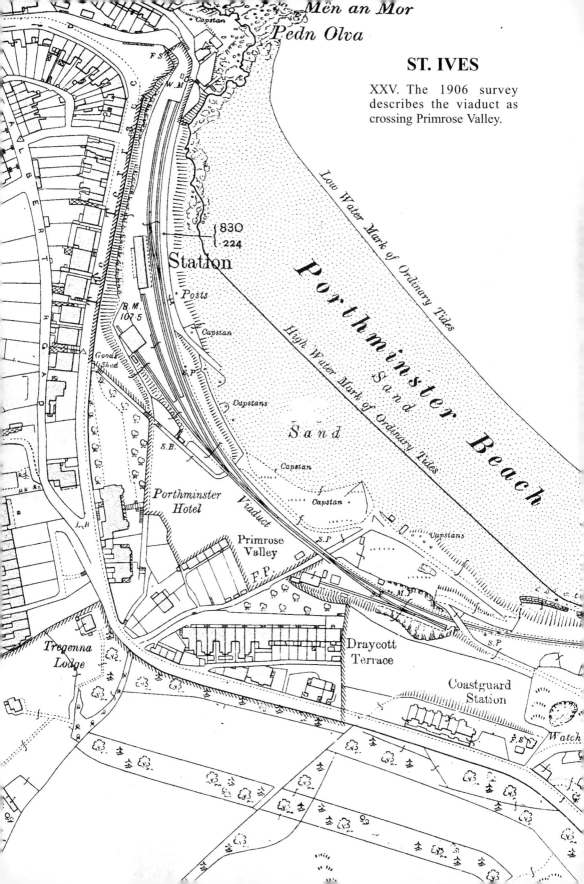

Mên an Mor

Pedn Olva

ST. IVES

XXV. The 1906 survey describes the viaduct as crossing Primrose Valley.

Low Water Mark of Ordinary Tides

830
224

Station

Posts

B.M. 107.5

Capstan

Good Shed

Capstans

Sand

High Water Mark of Ordinary Tides

Porthminster Beach

Porthminster Sand

S.B.

Porthminster Hotel

Viaduct

Primrose Valley

F.P.

Capstan

Capstan

S.P.

Capstans

M.P.

Draycott Terrace

Tregenna Lodge

Coastguard Station

S.P.

Watch

F.S.

112.   This postcard is from the broad gauge era. Soon after the narrowing in 1892, a third siding was provided, between the one shown and the goods shed. The platform was widened at that time, resulting in its edge no longer being under the border of the canopy. The GWR bought the nearby Tregenna Castle and converted it into an hotel in 1878. (Lens of Sutton)

Gt. Western Ry.   Gt. Western Ry.

St.IVES   St.IVES

TO

EXETER

Via Plymouth and Dawlish

10/11¼ PARLY.(3rd.Cls) 10/11¼

Issued subject to the conditions & regulations set out in the Company's Time Tables Books and Bills.   (H.G)

EXETER   EXETER

14.APR96

658

St. Ives	1903	1913	1923	1933
Passenger tickets issued	814	953	2582	2559
Season tickets issued	20887	18174	46862	23848
Parcels forwarded	*	*	617	1279
General goods forwarded (tons)	-	71	117	-
Coal and coke received (tons)	2208	1364	763	257
Other minerals received (tons)	2644	1908	1552	1424
General goods received (tons)	145	708	158	768
Trucks of livestock handled	9276	9575	13729	6200

(* not available.)

113.   On the right is the raised ticket collecting platform, which was in use until 1st January 1903. Beyond it is the original signal box, which was fitted with a new frame at that time. The engine shed and water tank are on the left. The fishing fleet stretches both sides of the viaduct, pilchards being its main catch. The takings at the station in its first 12 months were: passengers £1874, goods £3305 and fish £5245. Sadly, over-fishing almost destroyed the traffic.
(Lens of Sutton)

114. About 40 years later and we can note that the town had changed completely, the platform had been extended towards the signal box and the track in the foreground had been fitted with an apron to facilitate the washing out of cattle wagons. There was a staff of 17 for most of the 1930s and there were regular through coaches on the Cornish Riviera Express. (Lens of Sutton)

115. The third siding mentioned in caption 112 lasted only about five years, to be replaced by a loading dock. On it stands a six-ton crane, which replaced an eight-ton model in 1938. It is evident that the goods shed doorway was built for the broad gauge. No. 4563 was photographed in June 1956. (J.W.T.House/ C.L.Caddy)

116.   No. 4566 arrives from St. Erth on 21st August 1956 with a two-coach "B" set, plus an extra coach attached. The porter will apply the tail lamp as the guard removes the other one upon arrival. There was a camping coach here in 1958-59 and two from 1960-64, Summertime only. The hut on the left was for carriage cleaning equipment. (N.L.Browne)

117.   We now move to 27th September 1956, seasonal traffic is diminishing and so the extra coach can be left at the end of the line in case a sudden crowd arrives. Beyond the viaduct, the engine shed can be seen through the rain. The 20-lever signal box closed on 8th September 1963. (H.C.Casserley)

118.   Seen on the same day, the engine shed was in use until 8th September 1961. No. 4545 is being prepared for the train seen in the previous photograph. Goods service was withdrawn on 9th September 1963, but it had been provided by road since 1962. (H.C.Casserley)

119.   An August 1960 photo of no. 4564 reveals how narrow the platform became at its south end. Its length was still insufficient for the ten-coach through trains to and from Paddington on Summer Saturdays, which ran from 1956. They included a restaurant car. (R.C.Riley)

120.   Regular staffing ceased in May 1968 and a new station was opened on the site of the goods yard on 23rd May 1971. Following the success of the Lelant Saltings service, the platform was doubled in length in 1979, the new coping slabs being evident at both ends. Passengers in the "Skipper" on 22nd April 1986 are about to enjoy the scenic joys of the branch and will pass under the bridge on the left, only to feast on further fine vistas further south. (G.Gillham)

MP Middleton Press

Easebourne Lane, Midhurst, W Sussex. GU29 9AZ Tel: 01730 813169 Fax: 01730 812601
*If books are not available from your local transport stockist, order direct with cheque,
Visa or Mastercard, post free UK.*

BRANCH LINES

Branch Line to Allhallows
Branch Line to Alton
Branch Lines around Ascot
Branch Line to Ashburton
Branch Lines around Bodmin
Branch Line to Bude
Branch Lines around Canterbury
Branch Lines around Chard & Yeovil
Branch Line to Cheddar
Branch Lines around Cromer
Branch Lines to East Grinstead
Branch Lines of East London
Branch Lines to Effingham Junction
Branch Lines around Exmouth
Branch Lines to Falmouth, Helston & St. Ives
Branch Line to Fairford
Branch Lines around Gosport
Branch Line to Hawkhurst
Branch Lines to Horsham
Branch Lines around Huntingdon
Branch Line to Ilfracombe
Branch Line to Kingswear
Branch Line to Lambourn
Branch Lines to Launceston & Princetown
Branch Line to Looe
Branch Line to Lyme Regis
Branch Lines around Midhurst
Branch Line to Minehead
Branch Line to Moretonhampstead
Branch Lines to Newport
Branch Line to Newquay
Branch Lines around North Woolwich
Branch Line to Padstow
Branch Lines around Plymouth
Branch Lines to Seaton and Sidmouth
Branch Line to Selsey
Branch Lines around Sheerness
Branch Line to Shrewsbury
Branch Line to Swanage *updated*
Branch Line to Tenterden
Branch Lines around Tiverton
Branch Lines to Torrington
Branch Lines to Tunbridge Wells
Branch Line to Upwell
Branch Lines of West London
Branch Lines around Weymouth
Branch Lines around Wimborne
Branch Lines around Wisbech

NARROW GAUGE

Branch Line to Lynton
Branch Lines around Portmadoc 1923-46
Branch Lines around Porthmadog 1954-94
Branch Line to Southwold
Douglas to Port Erin
Kent Narrow Gauge
Northern France Narrow Gauge
Romneyrail
Southern France Narrow Gauge
Sussex Narrow Gauge
Two-Foot Gauge Survivors
Vivarais Narrow Gauge

SOUTH COAST RAILWAYS

Ashford to Dover
Bournemouth to Weymouth
Brighton to Worthing
Eastbourne to Hastings
Hastings to Ashford
Portsmouth to Southampton
Ryde to Ventnor
Southampton to Bournemouth

SOUTHERN MAIN LINES

Basingstoke to Salisbury
Bromley South to Rochester
Crawley to Littlehampton
Dartford to Sittingbourne
East Croydon to Three Bridges
Epsom to Horsham
Exeter to Barnstaple
Exeter to Tavistock
Faversham to Dover
London Bridge to East Croydon
Orpington to Tonbridge
Tonbridge to Hastings
Salisbury to Yeovil
Swanley to Ashford
Tavistock to Plymouth
Three Bridges to Brighton
Victoria to Bromley South
Victoria to East Croydon
Waterloo to Windsor
Waterloo to Woking
Woking to Portsmouth
Woking to Southampton
Yeovil to Exeter

EASTERN MAIN LINES

Ely to Kings Lynn
Fenchurch Street to Barking
Ipswich to Saxmundham
Liverpool Street to Ilford
Saxmundham to Yarmouth

WESTERN MAIN LINES

Ealing to Slough
Exeter to Newton Abbot
Newton Abbot to Plymouth
Newbury to Westbury
Paddington to Ealing
Plymouth to St. Austell
Slough to Newbury
St. Austell to Penzance

COUNTRY RAILWAY ROUTES

Andover to Southampton
Bath Green Park to Bristol
Bath to Evercreech Junction
Bournemouth to Evercreech Jn.
Cheltenham to Andover
Croydon to East Grinstead
Didcot to Winchester
East Kent Light Railway
Fareham to Salisbury

Guildford to Redhill
Reading to Basingstoke
Reading to Guildford
Redhill to Ashford
Salisbury to Westbury
Stratford upon Avon to Cheltenham
Strood to Paddock Wood
Taunton to Barnstaple
Wenford Bridge to Fowey
Westbury to Bath
Woking to Alton
Yeovil to Dorchester

GREAT RAILWAY ERAS

Ashford from Steam to Eurostar
Clapham Junction 50 years of change
Festiniog in the Fifties
Festiniog in the Sixties
Isle of Wight Lines 50 years of change
Railways to Victory 1944-46
Return to Blaenau 1970-82
SECR Centenary album
Talyllyn 50 years of change
Yeovil 50 years of change

LONDON SUBURBAN RAILWAYS

Caterham and Tattenham Corner
Charing Cross to Dartford
Clapham Jn. to Beckenham Jn.
Crystal Palace (HL) & Catford Loop
East London Line
Finsbury Park to Alexandra Palace
Kingston and Hounslow Loops
Lewisham to Dartford
Lines around Wimbledon
London Bridge to Addiscombe
Mitcham Junction Lines
North London Line
South London Line
West Croydon to Epsom
West London Line
Willesden Junction to Richmond
Wimbledon to Beckenham
Wimbledon to Epsom

STEAMING THROUGH

Steaming through Cornwall
Steaming through the Isle of Wight
Steaming through Kent
Steaming through West Hants
Steaming through West Sussex

TRAMWAY CLASSICS

Aldgate & Stepney Tramways
Barnet & Finchley Tramways
Bath Tramways
Brighton's Tramways
Bristol's Tramways
Burton & Ashby Tramways
Camberwell & W.Norwood Tramways
Clapham & Streatham Tramways
Croydon's Tramways

Dover's Tramways
East Ham & West Ham Tramways
Edgware and Willesden Tramways
Eltham & Woolwich Tramways
Embankment & Waterloo Tramway
Enfield & Wood Green Tramways
Exeter & Taunton Tramways
Greenwich & Dartford Tramways
Hammersmith & Hounslow Tramway
Hampstead & Highgate Tramways
Hastings Tramways
Holborn & Finsbury Tramways
Ilford & Barking Tramways
Kingston & Wimbledon Tramways
Lewisham & Catford Tramways
Liverpool Tramways 1. Eastern Routes
Liverpool Tramways 2. Southern Routes
Liverpool Tramways 3. Northern Routes
Maidstone & Chatham Tramways
Margate to Ramsgate
North Kent Tramways
Norwich Tramways
Portsmouth's Tramways
Reading Tramways
Seaton & Eastbourne Tramways
Shepherds Bush & Uxbridge Tramways
Southampton Tramways
Southend-on-sea Tramways
Southwark & Deptford Tramways
Stamford Hill Tramways
Twickenham & Kingston Tramways
Victoria & Lambeth Tramways
Waltham Cross & Edmonton Tramways
Walthamstow & Leyton Tramways
Wandsworth & Battersea Tramways

TROLLEYBUS CLASSICS

Bournemouth Trolleybuses
Croydon Trolleybuses
Derby Trolleybuses
Hastings Trolleybuses
Maidstone Trolleybuses
Portsmouth Trolleybuses
Reading Trolleybuses
Woolwich & Dartford Trolleybuses

WATERWAY ALBUMS

Kent and East Sussex Waterways
London to Portsmouth Waterway
West Sussex Waterways

MILITARY BOOKS

Battle over Portsmouth
Battle over Sussex 1940
Bombers over Sussex 1943-45
Bognor at War
Military Defence of West Sussex
Military Signals from the South Coast
Secret Sussex Resistance
Surrey Home Guard

OTHER RAILWAY BOOKS

Index to all Middleton Press stations
Industrial Railways of the South-East
South Eastern & Chatham Railways
London Chatham & Dover Railway
War on the Line (SR 1939-45)

BIOGRAPHIES

Garraway Father & Son
Mitchell & company